THE

Winston Churchill

BY
James Brown

·PARRAGON·

This edition first published by
Parragon Book Service Ltd in 1996

Parragon Book Service Ltd
Unit 13–17 Avonbridge Trading Estate
Atlantic Road, Avonmouth
Bristol BS11 9QD

Produced by Magpie Books,
an imprint of Robinson Publishing

ISBN 0 75251 557 8

A copy of the British Library Cataloguing in Publication
Data is available from the British Library.

Typeset by Whitelaw & Palmer Ltd, Glasgow
Printed in Singapore

EARLIEST DAYS

Winston Churchill was an aristocrat – an untitled one, to be sure, with a passionate belief in the rights and powers of the House of Commons, but an aristocrat for all that. He was the eldest son of Lord Randolph Churchill, MP, and the grandson of a duke. On his father's side he was descended from the great general, the first Duke of Marlborough, to whom a grateful nation had presented Blenheim Palace. There, on 30 November 1874, Winston Churchill was born.

His father was the third son of the seventh Duke;

his mother, Jennie, generally referred to as Lady Randolph, was the daughter of an American financier, Leonard Jerome. He was a sickly child. Thanks to his mother taking a tumble while out with a shooting party at Blenheim he had been born two months prematurely. He was brought up in the usual upper-class manner – which is to say, for the most part, by someone else: firstly his nanny, Mrs Everest, and then his teachers. His parents were remote figures. He later remarked that he had enjoyed no more than three or four real conversations with his father in his life.

He could at least count on the affection of Mrs Everest. Notwithstanding her forbidding name, his nanny was for some years the principal source of warmth in young Winston's life. He called her 'Ooms' or 'Oomany'.

His father's devotion to his political career seemed at times to preclude devotion to his young son, for whom he was a distant, and, in some measure, idealized figure. The climax of his

Winston in 1881

career was his appointment, in 1886, as Chancellor of the Exchequer in Lord Salisbury's Conservative administration. It was short-lived. In negotiating his first budget with his Cabinet colleagues, he threatened, in a letter to the Prime Minister, to resign if spending on the navy were not reduced. To his dismay Salisbury called his bluff, and took his letter as a resignation. He never held office again. For much of Churchill's childhood, his father was a frustrated, and sometimes embittered, man.

Perhaps it is understandable that Churchill should have been a troublesome child. His school reports tell of erratic talent. He was prone to bursts of temper. At his prep school he once seized the headmaster's venerable straw hat and kicked it to pieces.

He had been sent to prep school in Brighton. In one poignant letter home he wrote of his dismay at learning from the newspapers that his father – then still a minister – had been to Brighton, but had not come to see him. But his desire for his parents' attention did not necessarily make him tractable. Some of the letters between them reveal a struggle of wills, as the young Churchill insists that, while he is prepared to make an effort at school, he absolutely refuses to do any schoolwork in the holidays, where 'it would hang like a dark shadow over my pleasure'. Even at twelve he had a way with words – though he failed to persuade his mother on this occasion.

He worked enough to win a place at Harrow, whose salubrious situation it was hoped would suit his health. He arrived in 1888, and soon exercised his gift for words by learning a thousand lines of Macaulay's *Lays of Ancient Rome*, which won him a prize. In other areas of school life he fared less well. Its regimentation did not suit him: he was habitually late for classes, forgetful, and careless. It seems strange, therefore, that Lord Randolph should have decided that his son should go into the army class to prepare for the Royal Military College (as it then was; now the Royal Military Academy), Sandhurst. Apart from the young Churchill's unmilitary lack of discipline, he had hoped to go to university.

Though Lord Randolph did not think his son was up to studying at university, the Army was not an easy option. Preparation for Sandhurst's entrance exams required extra work. Churchill set to with a will, but his path was strewn with obstacles. For example, there was a master Churchill loathed, and whom he suspected of poisoning his mother's mind against him. The holidays, too, brought occasional disappointment, as when his parents had hired a house near Epsom, and declared it too full of visitors to the races for there to be room for their own son, who had to stay with relatives. Not surprisingly he stridently opposed the proposed dismissal of Mrs Everest when his younger brother, Jack, turned eleven, was deemed no longer to need her.

One bright spot in his school record came when he won the Harrow fencing competition, and then the public schools fencing championship. But it was followed by the setback of his failing the army exam. He resumed his labours, and retook the exam, only to fail again. He had improved, but not sufficiently.

He had come to the end of his schooldays. His next attempt to storm Sandhurst would be under the aegis of a 'crammer'. At his third attempt, he was finally accepted in 1893. He had not done well enough for the infantry, but his mark was good enough for the cavalry. He was understandably pleased, but his pleasure was short-lived.

Unknown to him, his father was already suffering from the disease that would kill him. The symptoms were mental as well as physical, and among them were fits of splenetic rage. One such coincided with the news of his son's success. He sent him a withering letter, in which

6

he told Churchill that his failure to get into the infantry indicated his 'slovenly happy-go-lucky harum scarum style of work'. He was 'among the 2nd & 3rd rate class who are only good for commissions in a cavalry regiment'. Lord Randolph finished with the threat to wash his hands of his son, for whom he predicted shameful failure. Churchill was devastated.

Lord Randolph rallied somewhat that autumn, and his relations with his son improved. Even so, it is easy to guess at the emotional needs that drove Churchill to protest again at the proposed dismissal of Mrs Everest from the Churchill family; this time, however, in vain.

His health continued to give concern, but he passed his first set of exams at Sandhurst. His father's condition, however, was parlous, and he became absolutely unapproachable. His wife decided he should travel, in the hope of recovery. When they got to Madras their doctor declared Lord Randolph had just six months to live, so they turned round and set off home again. At one point the patient became so crazed that he was put in a strait-jacket. Finally, at the end of 1894, they returned to London. Lord Randolph scarcely apprehended where he was. On 24 January 1895 he died; he was not quite forty-six years old.

YOUNG WINSTON

A few weeks after Lord Randolph's death Churchill became a second lieutenant in the 4th Queen's Own Hussars, and was sent to Aldershot. That summer brought a death that confirmed his putting aside childish things. Mrs Everest fell gravely ill. Churchill hastened to her side and was with her at the end. Writing to his mother he observed, 'I shall never know such a friend again.'

He already wanted to follow his father into politics, and started to prepare. He whiled away some idle hours at Aldershot reading his father's speeches and other political works, and set about

In the 4th Hussars, 1896

turning his job as a very junior officer into a launch-pad for a political career.

To this end he acquired a second string to his bow by becoming a journalist (for an officer, the British Army of the 1890s could be very generous with leave). As he travelled the globe, using family influence to get the exciting postings, he would be able to send back a stream of articles which would establish himself in the public eye. He started by reporting, for the *Daily Graphic*, on the Cuban rebellion of 1895, where he was attached to the Spanish forces and witnessed combat for the first time.

On his return, he was dismayed to find that his regiment had been posted to India. Being sent to one of the quieter parts of the Empire did not accord with his plans. From Bangalore he urged his mother to exert influence on the tame generals of her acquaintance to get him sent to Egypt, where a British force was engaged in retaking the Sudan from Mahdist rebels; or to have a newspaper employ him to cover a war between Greece and Turkey that broke out in April 1897. Without waiting for a reply he sailed for the war zone, only to find that the Turks had already won, so he proceeded to London.

Ironically, having been anxious not to go to India, Churchill then heard that a revolt had broken out on the North-West Frontier, and so sped back. General Sir Bindon Blood assigned him to 2 Brigade of the Malakand Field Force. In the lull before the storm he busied himself with reports for the *Daily Telegraph*. On 16 September 1897 the storm broke, and in the next four weeks Churchill was in action fifteen times. He saw colleagues fall, and himself killed several of the enemy. Sir Bindon was impressed. Churchill had more than glory on his mind, however; he wrote to his mother that his exploits ought to prove 'Quite a foundation for political life'.

Back in Bangalore he wrote a book about the

expedition. He had been frustrated that his pieces for the *Telegraph* had appeared anonymously, thus doing nothing to make his name. The book was to remedy this. *The Story of the Malakand Field Force* appeared in March 1898, although Churchill modestly omitted his personal exploits.

On leave in England in July, he addressed his first political meeting. His book also promoted his cause: the Prime Minister, Lord Salisbury, had been so impressed that he summoned the young author to Downing Street and promised to take an interest in his career. Churchill accordingly had himself posted to Egypt, attached to the 21st Lancers.

He arrived in Cairo on 2 August 1898. This time, besides his military duties, he was to write for the *Morning Post*. Almost immediately his unit set off up the Nile to confront the Dervishes, who, since the massacre of General Gordon and his garrison at Khartoum in 1885, had controlled almost all of the Sudan. Their leader, the Mahdi, had died only a few months after Gordon, but his successor, the Khalifa, Abdullah el-Taafi, had ruled the Sudan ever since. He now decided to give battle to the British forces. Major-General Sir Herbert Kitchener's army numbered 25,000; the Dervishes 40,000. At Omdurman, just outside Khartoum, and the site of the Mahdi's tomb, on 1 September the Dervishes turned to face the British.

That day, Churchill was scouting ahead. Climbing a hill, he suddenly beheld the enemy massed for attack. Early the following morning the sight was still more imposing: the enemy lines stretched for five miles. Having sent notes to Kitchener, Churchill remained with a few lancers, contemplating the spectacle. The Dervishes ignored him – until he rashly opened fire. He had to beat a swift retreat.

Soon the real battle commenced. Kitchener held

his cavalry back, so Churchill and the 21st Lancers were not ordered into action until after half-past eight. At 8.40 his unit mounted up and rode into the field. They saw what appeared to be an isolated group of some 150 spearmen, whom they charged. A rude surprise awaited them. The 'spearmen' proved to be riflemen, and Churchill found himself charging into a hail of bullets. He glanced behind him to check on his men, and when he looked ahead again, the isolated group of Dervishes had suddenly become a solid mass, at least a dozen men deep. These forces had been hidden in a ravine. In the furious struggle Churchill killed several men with his pistol which, because of a perhaps lucky injury, he had been forced to carry in place of the more usual sabre. By 9.15 the Dervishes were in retreat, and the 21st Lancers had crashed down into history in what proved to be one of the last – and wholly successful – cavalry charges.

Not all was glory and derring-do. Many had

perished; more were wounded. Great numbers of the enemy had been left to bleed to death on the battlefield. Churchill blamed Kitchener for the pitiless barbarity with which the British had conducted themselves in victory.

By the time the Sudan campaign ended, war loomed in South Africa. The Boers of the Transvaal and the Orange Free State, fiercely independent descendants of Dutch settlers, refused to submit to British authority. To South Africa Churchill hastened, this time out of uniform (having resigned his commission) as a reporter for the *Morning Post*. But that didn't stop him joining Captain Haldane, an old army friend, when, in 1899, the latter was sent in command of an armoured train into Boer territory. Still less did his theoretically non-combatant status deter him from lending a hand when the train was partially derailed and subjected to heavy Boer fire. Leaving his friend and some of the soldiers to return fire, Churchill organized and encouraged the driver and the stokers and as many of the soldiers as could be spared to shift the derailed wagons off the track, so that the engine could get away. He succeeded. There was not enough room for everyone on the engine, so he helped the wounded in, got in himself, and made off. Haldane had intended to make a stand with the fifty men who remained – a plan that was scotched when two of them spontaneously surrendered. Churchill had got safely away, but, apprised of Haldane's plan, walked back to assist. The Boers arrested him.

Churchill protested at being made a prisoner of war. He showed his press credentials, and pointed out that he had been unarmed when caught – though this was only because he'd forgotten to pick his pistol up again after having used it as a hammer on a recalcitrant coupling earlier in the day. To no avail. The Boers had seen his heroism, and it had deprived them of an engine they had wanted for themselves. So he passed his twenty-fifth birthday in a prison camp in Pretoria.

There he was reunited with Haldane and, togeth-

Churchill in a Boer prison camp

er with one Sergeant-Major Brockie, who spoke Dutch, they planned to escape. In the event, only Churchill got away. He walked off into Pretoria, unable to speak the language, and 300 miles from safety. After further adventures – jumping from a train and stumbling upon sympathizers who hid him down a mine – Churchill was smuggled back into British-held territory hidden under bales of wool. Once safe, he had a bath and a change of clothes and then made the gentlemanly gesture of telegraphing the Boer authorities, 'Escape not due to any fault of your guards.'

He proceeded by sea to Durban, and from there back to the area just south of Ladysmith, where he had been captured, in order to report on General Sir Radvers Buller's progress against the Boers. Buller was so impressed by the reporter's pluck that he gave him a commission in the South African Light Horse. Churchill was soldier and journalist again. After seeing action several more times, he finally embarked for England on 7 July, 1900.

FIRST TASTE OF POWER

Within a week of his homecoming Churchill visited Oldham, where he had earlier fought an unsuccessful by-election, to confirm that he would again stand there as a Conservative. He had not long to wait. The voters of Oldham went to the polls on 1 October 1900. It was a near-run thing, but Churchill was one of the two MPs elected.

On 14 February 1901, barely three weeks after Queen Victoria's death, he took his seat in the House of Commons. From the first he found himself at odds with his party. He criticized protectionist policies, whereby Britain used its imperial power to secure unfair economic advantage. Soon he also made his voice heard in opposition to the Government's high spending on the military, the very issue which had ended his father's political career.

As he developed his position, he became an increasingly outspoken proponent of Free Trade, a key Liberal policy. A Liberal who heard him speak in Birmingham late in 1903 commented, 'That man may call himself what he likes but he's no more a Tory than I am.' Churchill's political sympathies became so well known that, notwithstanding his being a Tory, he was invited to stand as a Liberal in Manchester. On 31 May 1904 the break with the Tories came: he entered the House, glanced at both sides, bowed to the Speaker, and took a place on the Opposition benches.

The following year brought good fortune to his new party. Just after Churchill's thirtieth birthday, Arthur Balfour, the Conservative

Winston Churchill MP, 1904

Prime Minister, played a desperate political gamble. He resigned in the hope that the Liberals would prove too disunited to form a government. He was wrong. The Liberals won, their leader Sir Henry Campbell-Bannerman, becoming Prime Minister.

Churchill had made a great impression, and Campbell-Bannerman rewarded him with his first ministerial office: Under-Secretary of State at the Colonial Office.

In the several offices he was to hold over the next few years, Churchill displayed a concern for social welfare. Much as he favoured competition, he also believed in the need for a safety net for the unfortunate. However, it was not just social conscience that impelled him to seek high office. It was also a temperamental need. As he had once relished adventure, so now he needed the excitement of power. Without it, and occasionally even with it, he could fall prey to bouts of depression.

Sometimes he found the means to combine his duties with his lust for adventure. In 1907 he embarked on a long trip around Africa as Under-Secretary for the Colonies, and indulged himself in the white man's sport of big-game hunting.

Back in London further advancement awaited him. In April 1908 the Prime Minister, Campbell-Bannerman, resigned because of ill health, dying only three weeks later. His Chancellor of the Exchequer, Herbert Asquith took over, and in the ensuing reshuffle Churchill, then still only thirty-three, entered the Cabinet as President of the Board of Trade. It was a post that would give him scope to implement some of his ideas for social reform. But his assumption of office did not go smoothly. The procedure then observed, required a newly appointed Cabinet minister to seek re-election. This Churchill did, and lost his North-West Manchester seat, for which he had become Liberal MP in 1906. He was out of the

Commons for just over a fortnight before being elected MP for Dundee.

In office he embarked on reforms. He instituted an arbitration service to resolve industrial disputes; he sought to establish a network of Labour Exchanges to help the unemployed back into work and to enable the government to determine the real need for benefits; he tried to improve the working conditions of the miners.

Outside Parliament his private life was changing. He had first met Clementine Hozier in 1904 at a party, and where he had disconcerted her by his steady, silent gaze. They had met again in 1908, when he had promised to send her a copy of his life of Lord Randolph (which had been published in 1906) – a promise he then failed to keep. However, their relationship blossomed. He invited her to Blenheim with the idea of proposing. Touchingly, though he was then the most successful politician of his generation and a man of proven bravery, it took him two days to pluck up the courage. They were married on 12 September 1908 in St Margaret's, Westminster.

After honeymooning in Italy, Churchill returned to work. He wanted to establish a state-run and subsidized system of unemployment benefit and a statutory minimum wage. Both his plans and the Government itself were under threat, however, a constitutional crisis lay just around the corner. The House of Lords was overwhelmingly Conservative, and was so dismayed at the 1909 budget presented by David Lloyd George (then Chancellor of the Exchequer), that it threatened to throw it out. It was doubtful whether they had the right to do so but – since Britain's constitution is unwritten – the only way to test it was to try.

The immediate result was the general election of 1910, though in the event it solved little. The Liberals were returned to power, but again as a minority government, dependent upon support from the Irish Liberal Party. Churchill became

With Lloyd George, 1910

Home Secretary. He got sucked into the thick of the constitutional crisis when Asquith called upon him to present the Government's proposals for restructuring the Lords. The plans were shelved when, on 6 May 1910, King Edward VII died, since it was felt unfair to the new king, George V, to try to resolve constitutional questions, in which the monarch plays a central role, immediately after his succession. When at last the plans were taken up again the underlying problem remained intractable. Another general election followed, within a year of the last, but the outcome was again inconclusive.

It was also a period of unrest in the country at large. As Home Secretary, Churchill was responsible for maintaining public order during a series of strikes. Time and again he showed himself loath to use military force to restore order, and preferred wherever possible to use only the police, for which some criticized him. When he felt he could do so without

Clementine and Winston, 1912

undermining the government's authority, he was willing to hold talks with the strikers. These were hardly policies to endear him to the Conservative opposition, yet he actively sought rapprochement between the two parties, seeking to find some common ground such as might ease the continuing constitutional crisis. In the Commons, however, he remained the *bête noire* of the Conservatives. Outside the House, he could console himself with the joys of parenthood. His first child, Diana, had been born in July 1909, his second, Randolph, was born in May 1911. The secure foundation of family life may have contributed to the evenness of temper with which he continued to seek co-operation with the opposition, Parliamentary uproar notwithstanding.

In August 1911, the Lords finally accepted that they had not the right to veto money bills sent to them from the Commons. No sooner had this truce been achieved, than industrial unrest broke out again. That month saw a dock strike all round Britain, soon followed by a railway strike. Rioting ensued. Churchill's was the difficult job of using just enough force to restore order, but not so much as to provoke further upheaval.

However, by the end of the year his attention shifted to the international scene. Germany had long been building up its military power. Churchill himself had witnessed its armies on manoeuvres. Among Germany's ambitions was a desire for a port on the Atlantic. In July 1911 it tried to secure a naval base in Agadir in Morocco, sending the gunboat *Panther* to back up its claim. Under diplomatic pressure Germany finally climbed down in November. However, the incident alerted Churchill to the work that needed to be done for the Royal Navy to ready it in case of war with Germany. He persuaded Asquith to make him First Lord of the Admiralty.

CHURCHILL AT WAR: 1914-1918

The outbreak of the First World War found Churchill well prepared. He had foreseen the conflict, and had used his powers as First Lord to do all he could to stiffen Britain's defences.

In the ominous summer of 1914, on 28 June, Archduke Franz Ferdinand, the nephew and heir of Franz Joseph, Emperor of Austro–Hungaria, was assassinated by a Serb nationalist in Sarajevo, as was his wife. At the instigation of the German Kaiser, Wilhelm II, Austro-Hungaria delivered an ultimatum to Serbia, which Churchill described to his wife as 'the most insolent document of its kind ever devised'. It was manifestly designed to provoke war. Such was the system of alliances that divided the continent into two armed camps, that soon almost all Europe would be at war.

Austro-Hungaria invaded Serbia on 28 July. Germany declared war on Serbia's ally, Russia, and then on 3 August demanded that Belgium allow its troops right of passage to invade France, Russia's ally. Britain, ally of both Russia and France, was pledged to defend Belgian neutrality, and sent Germany an ultimatum. This was ignored. As of midnight on 4 August 1914, Britain and Germany were at war.

Briefly, Churchill was involved in doomed attempts that October to hold Antwerp against the German invaders. Back at the Admiralty, he recalled Admiral Lord ('Jackie') Fisher from retirement to serve under him as First Sea Lord. Fisher was a brilliant, but erratic man. Churchill relished the older man's capacity for boldly

Churchill and Lord 'Jackie' Fisher

unconventional plans, but in giving him a position of such prominence, he was taking a risk.

Early in 1915, soon after the Western Front had been established, the opposing forces stabilizing in a line running from the Swiss frontier to the Belgian coast, Churchill began to rack his brains to see if some other front could be opened up that might bring victory at a lower price. In November 1914 Turkey had sided with Germany and Austro-Hungaria (as had Bulgaria in October), and Churchill was much attracted by the idea of striking at Turkey. Victory in that quarter would free thousands of British troops in Egypt and the Middle East, which could then be switched to the assault on the Austro-Hungarian Empire. Deprived of its allies, Germany would surely capitulate. Thus the scheme for an attack on the Dardanelles thus threatening Constantinople, the capital of the Ottoman Empire, was born.

It was dogged by difficulties. Kitchener,

Churchill's erstwhile commander in Egypt, now Secretary of State for War, seemed incapable of making up his mind whether he could or should provide support from the Army. Thanks to the vacillation of his colleagues, action was often postponed. But that was not the only obstacle. The initial attempt in March 1915 by 'ships alone' was a costly failure, Turkish shore batteries and mines taking a heavy toll of the Allied fleet. Successive admirals on the spot, to whom Churchill felt obliged to give some latitude, repeatedly failed to press the attack. By the time of the ill-fated Gallipoli landings on 25 April, the whole scheme had effectively been removed from Churchill's control. The Allies established footholds on the peninsula, but all attempts to drive the Turks out were defeated, often with dreadful casualties on both sides. By 9 January 1916, the entire Allied force had been withdrawn. Much of the blame for the failure fell upon Churchill.

In his own department, Fisher's attitude was

Back in the army, with his second-in-command,
France, 1916

impossible to predict. Matters came to a head when the First Sea Lord, who had several times threatened to resign over various issues, and who disapproved of the naval attempt to force the Dardanelles, resigned on 15 May and vanished from the scene. Asquith felt himself to be under intolerable pressure from the Conservative opposition, for whom Fisher's resignation was powerful ammunition. He offered them a share in a coalition government. Their price was the removal of Churchill from the Admiralty.

For a time Churchill retained his place on Asquith's War Council, and, though unable to control the campaign in the Dardanelles, continued to play a part. However, he was increasingly isolated. Finally he abandoned politics, and on 18 November 1916 donned uniform again and made for the Western Front where, as a lieutenant-colonel, he took command of a battalion of the Royal Scots Fusiliers.

However, he continued to hanker after political

life. Since he was still an MP he could speak in the Commons. In March and April 1917 he attended parliamentary debates while on leave, and when, after the costly Battle of Arras, his tragically depleted battalion was merged with another, he sought leave to resume his political duties permanently. On 7 May he bade his men farewell.

Back in London he sought to clear himself of blame over the Dardanelles fiasco, which entailed exposing Kitchener's unhelpful role. On 6 June Kitchener was drowned when HMS *Hampshire*, *en route* for Russia, hit a mine and sank, thus making it impossible to call him to account. Asquith, after some dithering, also forbade Churchill to use any of the official documents. Churchill was overlooked in the reshuffle occasioned by Kitchener's death.

Asquith himself was not to hold office much longer. Senior colleagues were dissatisfied with him, and on 5 December three of them resigned from the Government. Asquith had no option but to resign (as did his principal Liberal colleagues), and was replaced by Lloyd George. Still there was no place for Churchill: the Government remained a coalition and the Conservatives would not countenance his return. However, Lloyd George valued him, and from May 1917 routinely sought his advice. Finally on 16 July, he bit the bullet and asked Churchill to become Minister of Munitions. Howls of Tory outrage went up, and were only quelled by Lloyd George threatening to resign himself.

1918 witnessed last desperate thrusts on both sides in the struggle to break the stalemate on the Western Front. Late in 1917, torn by revolution, Russia had agreed an armistice with the Central Powers, freeing a large number of troops for the war against Britain and France. Germany knew she must defeat the Allies before the armies of America, which had declared war on the Central Powers in April 1917, could swing the balance in the Allies' favour. The German offensive began in March. By degrees the advance slackened, slowed and halted, and the last great Allied counter-offensive, now supported by fresh and eager US troops, began. By August the tide of war had changed.

The enemy alliance fragmented. First Bulgaria surrendered, then Turkey, then the Austro-Hungarian Empire, and finally, on 7 November, Germany sought an armistice. A few days later the Kaiser fled to Holland, and the armistice was agreed. The guns fell silent on 11 November.

CHURCHILL IN AND
OUT OF GOVERNMENT

Four days later Churchill's fourth child, Marigold, was born, but he could not linger long at his wife's side, for ten days after that Lloyd George called a snap election to establish support for continued coalition government. He triumphed at the polls, although the greater number of the Government's majority were Coalition Conservatives. Churchill retained his Dundee seat.

Though the war with Germany was over, some 14,000 British troops were still in action in Russia, supporting the White Russians against

the revolutionary forces. Having gone there
with weapons to help the Tsarist regime fight
Germany, they had become embroiled in the
civil strife that followed the Tsar's abdication
and the Bolshevik revolution of November
1917. As the opportunity for decisive inter-
vention seemed to present itself, Churchill
would bombard the Prime Minister with urgent
requests for a change of policy. However, by
November 1919 the Bolsheviks had triumphed,
by which time all British forces had been
brought home.

There were violent troubles nearer home. In
Ireland, after the Easter Rising of 1916 in
Dublin the campaign for Irish independence had
become more hard-line. The election had
delivered success to the Irish Republican party,
Sinn Féin, at the expense of the Irish Party.
Many of the new Republican Irish MPs refused
to go to Westminster, and instead met at Dublin
where they announced that they were now the
true government of Ireland. To make real this

claim, Irish nationalists set about making Ireland ungovernable by the British authorities. In this emergency Churchill lent qualified support to the reinforcement of the police with the now infamous 'Black and Tans', volunteers for the auxiliary arm of the Royal Irish Constabulary, their name deriving from their mixed uniform of khaki service dress and the dark green of the RIC. These were mostly battle-hardened ex-servicemen, whose notion of justice, so far as it existed at all, was summary. Rather than enforce the law, they inflicted reprisals, culminating in their destroying much of Cork in December 1920 to avenge the death of one of their own. The Irish police were also backed by the British Army, but they found a formidable and ruthless opponent in the Irish Republican Army.

The New Year of 1921 brought Churchill new duties. On 7 January he became Colonial Secretary. Lloyd George charged him with making economies in the British administration of the Middle East. He journeyed to Egypt, and held a conference, which sought to confer upon the Arab states a degree of independence on condition that they respect Jewish settlement in Palestine. The economies were not forthcoming. The opposition of Zionism and Arab nationalism remains largely unresolved today.

Back in England personal grief awaited Churchill. His mother died on 13 June at the age of sixty-seven. She had twice remarried, but was interred next to Lord Randolph. Tragedy followed when his infant daughter, Marigold, contracted meningitis that August, and died on the 24th.

Ireland figured among Churchill's responsibilities, and he now pursued a more conciliatory course than he had done before, and played a leading role in negotiations with the Irish nationalists, who wanted an independent Ireland, and loyalist Ulstermen, who wanted no part of it. He personally conducted the talks with Arthur Griffith and Michael Collins, the great

IRA leader, which led to the conclusion of the Anglo-Irish Treaty in December 1921. The greater part of Ireland (thenceforth the Irish Free State) would become a dominion – that is, it would be self-governing, but George V would remain its sovereign. So bitterly was the compromise with Britain resented by hard-line Republicans that the fledgeling state was soon riven by civil war.

The Conservatives chafed at Irish independence, and their subordination to the Coalition rankled with them. A crisis in the Near East over Turkish ambitions gave them the excuse they needed to topple the government. On 19 October 1922 they withdrew support from Lloyd George, who resigned that afternoon.

On 18 October Churchill had been operated on for appendicitis. He struggled back to consciousness the following day just long enough to read the papers and find that he was no longer in office. The new Prime Minister, Andrew Bonar

Law, lost no time in calling an election, which returned him and a purely Conservative government. Churchill's convalescence all but precluded campaigning in his Dundee constituency, and he lost his seat. 'In the twinkling of an eye I found myself without an office, without a party and without an appendix.'

He took a much-needed holiday and set about refurbishing Chartwell, the country house in Kent that he had bought that year. Stanley Baldwin, who in May 1923 succeeded Bonar Law as Prime Minister and Tory leader, called another election in December, campaigning on a protectionist platform. Churchill stood as a Liberal for West Leicester, and spoke out for Free Trade. He was not elected.

Besides devoting more time to his writing – for Churchill continued to publish books at a rate that would have exhausted most other people – he began to reassess his political position. The advance of the Labour Party touched a nerve of

unreasoning animosity in him. He urged that
Liberals and Conservatives make common cause
against socialism. When instead the Liberals
joined in coalition with the Labour Party in
January 1924 to oust the Tories from power, and
make the Labour leader, Ramsay MacDonald,
Prime Minister, Churchill's disillusion with his
party grew. In a by-election in Westminster in
1924 he stood as an Independent, losing to the
Conservative by the narrowest of margins. His
rapprochement with his original party continued,
and Baldwin agreed that when next he stood he
should present himself as a 'Constitutionalist', and
thus enjoy official Conservative support. Under
this banner he offered himself to the voters of
Epping at the General Election of 29 October
1924. He was returned with a majority of 9,000.
In the country at large, the Conservatives swept
the board with 419 MPs, the Liberal Party secur-
ing a mere 40 seats. Somewhat to Churchill's surprise, Baldwin invited him to become Chancellor
of the Exchequer. He promptly rejoined the
Conservative Party and took office.

His policies showed that he had not deserted his Liberal principles. He embarked on social reform, pressing for cuts in naval spending to help pay for it. He extended the availability of pensions to widows and orphans, and lightened the burden of taxation upon the poorest. By his own lights, he aimed at 'the appeasement of class bitterness', but when he felt industrial unrest threatened the state, he was an implacable foe. During the General Strike of May 1926, Churchill assumed responsibility for a government newspaper to keep the public informed and to counteract scaremongering. The *British Gazette* castigated the strike as a challenge to the state. The more extreme side of Churchill was manifested in his proposals to take over the BBC and guard food convoys into the capital with machine-guns and armoured cars.

On 12 May the TUC called the General Strike off: it was too costly. Churchill's conciliatory side now emerged in his efforts to resolve the continuing dispute between miners and mine owners. He sought a way forward, only to find himself blocked by the owners and by the lack of political will in the Cabinet to support arbitration. Churchill's wry comment on the business was that he'd supposed the miners to be the most unreasonable people he had ever met, until he met the mine owners.

Churchill resumed his normal duties as Chancellor. He presented his third, fourth and fifth budgets to the house, attracting plaudits for his powers of oratory. And he continued to write, publishing between 1923 and 1931 successive volumes of his First World War history, *The World Crisis*.

The Conservatives lost the election of May 1929. Churchill held his seat, but was out of office. He was not to re-enter government for another ten years.

A VOICE CRYING IN THE WILDERNESS

Over the next few years Churchill became disillusioned with politics, and found himself increasingly at odds with his own party. He challenged its support of the Labour Government's plans to give India Dominion status, for which he considered they were not ready, and resigned from the Shadow Cabinet over the issue in 1931. He concentrated upon lecturing tours and writing (in 1930 he published his enthralling volume of autobiography, *My Early Life*), partly to provide for his family and make good his losses in the Wall Street Crash of October 1929, which brought America's

Depression to Europe. When, in 1931, Baldwin decided to go into coalition with the Labour Party and form a 'National' government under Ramsay MacDonald to deal with the economic crisis, there was no post for Churchill.

One cause, however, tempted him to remain in politics. He began to grow concerned about Germany. These concerns deepened when Adolf Hitler became Chancellor of Germany on 30 January 1933, and promptly arrogated further powers to himself. However, the British government was set upon disarmament as the surest way to keep the peace in Europe. Assiduously, Churchill began to gather evidence of German rearmament, and of the inadequacy of British forces, arms and diplomacy. Strength alone would give the Germans pause. This would be his persistent theme until the eve of war itself, and his own party leadership would shun him for it. Undeterred, he carried his appeal beyond the Commons to the country at large, by radio broadcasts and by newspaper articles. Always his message was that it was not war he sought, but the way to avoid war.

In June 1935, MacDonald resigned the premiership. He was ill. Baldwin replaced him. There was no office for Churchill, though Baldwin did invite him to sit on the Air Defence Research Sub-Committee.

The Conservatives won the election of November 1935 decisively. Churchill's warnings had proved to be sufficiently true, and touched such a nerve in the party, that he expected to be recalled to office. No call came. Baldwin explained his overlooking Churchill to a friend, 'If there is going to be war – and no one can say there is not – we must keep him fresh to be our war Prime Minister.' Churchill continued to warn of the dangers of inadequate preparation, rallying support from as a wide a spectrum of opinion as possible through such bodies as the Anti-Nazi Council. He also took the side of King Edward VIII (one of the few in the House

At the Coronation review of the fleet

of Commons who did) during the Abdication crisis of December 1936, occasioned by the King's desire to marry a divorced American commoner, which resulted in Edward's abdication in favour of his brother, who became King George VI.

In May 1937 Baldwin retired from office, and was succeeded as Prime Minister by Neville Chamberlain. The Goverment's policy of appeasement proceeded in the teeth of Churchill's warnings. In September 1938 Germany mobilised. Hitler made specious claims to the Sudetenland, a Czech territory inhabited by German-speaking people. Twice that month Chamberlain flew to meet Hitler, and helped to formulate a plan to transfer the Sudetenland to the Reich. Naively he reported back to his Cabinet that he was 'satisfied that Herr Hitler would not go back on his word once he had given it'. On 29 September 1938, he flew to meet Hitler and representatives of France and Italy at Munich. Between them they agreed the transfer of the contested territory to Germany, and presented this as a *fait accompli* to the Czechs. Chamberlain returned, proclaiming 'Peace in our time', and brandishing the agreement. Chamberlain's diplomacy was popular – for the time being. Churchill saw the Munich Agreement as an 'unmitigated defeat'.

On 15 March 1939, German forces invaded Czechoslovakia and occupied Prague. Chamberlain pledged that Britain would defend Poland, as did the French Prime Minister, Edouard Daladier. Churchill's standing rose as the truth about Nazism became palpable. Eventually, under pressure, Chamberlain agreed to one of the measures Churchill urged, the establishment of a Ministry of Supply. But Churchill was not to be the minister; he remained on the back benches.

On 23 August Germany and Russia had signed, in secret, a mutual agreement of non-aggression, the Nazi-Soviet Pact, by which the two countries effectively divided territories in Eastern Europe between them.

The feeling in government circles, and among the public, that Churchill ought to be in office gathered force. On 25 August Britain allied herself with Poland; on 31 August Hitler invaded that country from the west, as did the Russians from the east. The Commons was recalled. Chamberlain privately asked Churchill to join his War Cabinet. Bizarrely, he then did nothing further, and Churchill was left expecting a call that never came. The Cabinet decided to send Hitler an ultimatum, but Chamberlain delayed, and was only forced into action by the demands of his own ministers. The ultimatum was sent on 3 September, as was one from France. They were ignored by the Germans.

That evening, Chamberlain broadcast to the nation that Britain was at war with Germany. The same afternoon he had appointed Churchill First Lord of the Admiralty – the post

49

he had filled at the outbreak of the First World War. Churchill became anxious to intercept supplies of iron ore going to Germany from neutral Sweden. At the same time he was himself a formidable weapon in the struggle to maintain morale, and several times he broadcast to the nation. Another struggle, to get his Cabinet colleagues to contemplate decisive action, proved more frustrating, and months elapsed without their agreeing to any of Churchill's plans. By the time they were ready to act so too was Hitler, and to deadlier effect, for in April 1940 he seized Denmark and occupied Oslo and other sections of the Norwegian coast.

Chamberlain's reputation plummeted. On 7 May in the Commons he suffered a protest so disconcerting and from many in his own party, that he determined to form a coalition government of national unity. The Labour Party, however, were adamant that they would not serve under him. Early on 10 May German

The new Prime Minister, May 1940

forces invaded Belgium, Holland and France. By the end of the day Churchill was Prime Minister.

HIS FINEST HOUR

For the next five years Churchill inspired the British people, and sustained the spirits of his advisers and colleagues, whom he sometimes also drove to distraction. Such was Britain's plight that there could be few successes at first; endurance would be all. Germany was prepared for war; Britain was not. He strove to nerve the French to continue to resist as German armoured divisions swept around the Maginot Line, static defences in which France had placed too great a faith. The resolve of the French leaders faltered under the onslaught. British forces in Northern France were cut off, and had to be evacuated from Dunkirk by the Royal

Navy and a flotilla of small vessels. By the time the operation ended on 3 June, over 200,000 British and 100,000 French troops had escaped to safety, although all their heavy equipment was lost. Others had sacrificed themselves to make the evacuation possible. At the end of June the French sought an armistice. Marshal Philippe Petain, one of the leading French commanders in the First World War, formed a government for what became Vichy France, Vichy being the new government's capital. The administration was effectively a puppet of the Germans, who occupied some one-half of the country until 1942, when they occupied the remainder.

In an attempt to wipe out the country's air defences, as a prelude to a planned invasion, the *Luftwaffe* launched wave after wave of attacks upon Britain, starting on 10 July 1940. Its strength far exceeded that of the RAF. On 16 August Churchill went to Uxbridge to follow the battle in one of Fighter Command's operation rooms. Impressed by the fighter pilots' gallantry in this seemingly unequal struggle, as he came away he uttered words that would later be incorporated in his speech on the battle, 'Never in the field of human conflict has so much been owed by so many to so few'. By the end of the month 'the many' tasted war for themselves: the Blitz had begun. Bombs rained down upon cities almost nightly, claiming the lives of nearly 7000 civilians that September. But the *Luftwaffe* did not have it all its own way, suffering heavy losses in men and machines. By the middle of September it was clear that the Germans could no longer maintain the intensity of the air assault. Any hopes of an invasion of Britain began to evaporate.

Churchill sought American aid; without it there would be little chance of carrying the war to the enemy. Early in 1941 the idea of Lend-Lease emerged from his talks with President Franklin D. Roosevelt's representative: Britain could lease matériel from the USA, and the payments would be deferred until after the war.

There remained the problem of transporting supplies across the Atlantic. U-boats prowled the ocean, lurking in the depths, ready to strike at the convoys that pumped the blood of food, weapons and ammunition, machine tools, and hundreds of other vital supplies into Britain's war effort.

On land the Germans made gains that April in the Balkans and in Greece. They were still formidable in the air – the Blitz against Britain continued.

Then Hitler gambled. He had maintained that it would be folly to open a war on two fronts. That was why before hostilities began he had concluded the non aggression pact with Stalin. But in June 1941, eager to gain oil from the Caucasus, and fired by the ideological abyss between Nazism and Communism, he invaded Russia. Churchill immediately set his fiercely anti-communist sentiments to one side, and supported Stalin's war-effort. Unable yet to relieve the pressure on the Russian front by making landings in Western Europe, he arranged supplies to the hard-pressed USSR. From August 1941, thanks to the code-breakers at Bletchley, Churchill could also give Stalin valuable information about German plans.

Tirelessly, and often at considerable personal risk, he crossed and recrossed the Atlantic to meet President Roosevelt, at first to argue for the entry of the USA into the war, and then, in the wake of the Japanese surprise attack on the American naval base at Pearl Harbor in the Pacific on 7 December 1941, to ensure that the European theatre received priority. Hitler obliged in this by – somewhat needlessly – declaring war on the USA.

Churchill's health suffered. At the White House, having addressed the Houses of Congress on 26 December, he suffered a mild heart attack. He was at work the following day. Back home early in 1942 anxieties mounted. The war was now

A wartime broadcast

being fought on a bewildering number of fronts: by resistance movements in Western Europe and th Balkans, in the Middle East, in North Africa, in the Atlantic, in the Mediterranean, in the Far East and throughout the Pacific, in Russia and the Ukraine. The burden on Churchill's shoulders was heavy, and sometimes disappointments bowed him down. One such was the fall of Tobruk in a North African campaign that had swung back and forth along the coast like a pendulum. In August 1942 he decided to give command of the African campaign to Leiutenant-General Bernard Montgomery. Montgomery was not noted for the sweetness of his temper, but as Churchill explained to his wife, 'If he's disagreeable to those about him, he is also disagreeable to the enemy.' By the end of October Churchill's faith was repaid: Montgomery and the Eighth Army had beaten Rommel and the *Africakorps* at El Alamein. By November Montgomery had consolidated the first great Allied victory of the war: Rommel's German and Italian forces were in disarray, and were retreating as best they could westwards, where British and American forces had landed and were waiting for them. On 13 November Tobruk was retaken.

Churchill kept up a punishing pace, visiting the different theatres of war, and meeting his allies. He had established a working relationship with Stalin, but remained deeply concerned about the post-Nazi future. As the tide turned on the Eastern Front, the possibility of leaving Europe under a communist tyranny scarcely less terrible than the Nazi regime haunted him. The case of Poland presented the problem in acute form. The freedom and integrity of Poland were among the causes for which the Allies had gone to war, but the country was too close to Russia for Churchill to bring effective pressure to bear to dissuade Stalin from installing a puppet communist regime in due course. Stalin promised a free Poland, within borders further to the west than they had been before the war, but promises are cheap for those who do not mean to keep them.

The V for Victory sign

In July 1943 the war was carried to the homeland of one of the Axis powers, by the invasion of Sicily. Italian resistance crumbled at first, and the country's dictator, Benito Mussolini, fell from power. But Nazi forces swung south, occupied much of the Italian mainland, and, extracting Mussolini from the mountain refuge in which the Italians, after their surrender, had kept him under house arrest, established him as their puppet in northern Italy. The Italian campaign became a grim affair, and Churchill was obliged to intercede with his American allies to ensure that the resources necessary to its success were not prematurely diverted to the Pacific, or to the accumulations for the invasion of mainland Europe.

By the end of 1943 Churchill was again ill. He had been dogged by pneumonia, which returned to plague him in December, confining him to his bed in Carthage in Tunisia, where his tireless travelling had taken him. He reassured his daughter, Sarah, 'If I die, don't worry – the war is won.' A few days later he suffered a second heart attack. Yet within a week he was up and about in his dressing gown, conferring with British and American commanders.

Finally in June 1944, the Allies were ready to begin the liberation of Europe, for which Churchill had long planned. On D-Day, 6 June 1944, Allied troops invaded Normandy from the sea and the air. Churchill was not far behind. On 12 June he too clambered ashore, and on coming away again in a warship took delight in encouraging the captain to 'have a plug' at the enemy before they left.

The Nazis were far from finished, however. That same month they launched the first of the V-1 flying bombs at Britain. But Churchill was already thinking ahead, trying to secure a peace that would be worth fighting for. He visited Stalin, with whom he held talks in the hope of saving from Stalinism some of the countries that lay in the Red Army's path as it fought its way westward to Berlin. The main concession he won was that Russian interest in Greece should be less than that of the West. Though his health continued uncertain, on Christmas Eve 1944 Churchill tore himself away from his family, who had hoped at least to spend Christmas with him, and flew to Greece. The Greeks had maintained a guerrilla war against the occupying Germans from April 1941 until Athens was liberated by the British in October 1944. Now, however, the rival partisan groups were at war with each other for control of the country, with British troops often caught between the two sides. There was no clear government; communist guerrillas were fighting the monarchists in a struggle for power, which, in 1946, would eventually explode into civil war. Churchill flew straight into the war zone, cheered by the dangers that caused his family terrible anxiety. On Boxing Day he was in the comparative safety of HMS *Ajax* off the Greek coast, when the communists started shelling the area. In the midst of dictation Churchill exclaimed as a shell exploded near by, 'There – you bloody well missed us! Come on, try again.'

Having done what he could in Greece, Churchill looked ahead to the most important summit meeting of the war. Stalin announced that his doctors would not let him leave the USSR, so Churchill, whose health was far from robust, and Roosevelt, who was, as it turned out, mortally ill, had to travel to Yalta, in the Crimea. The meeting convened in February 1945. Roosevelt was too sick to be an effective contributor, while Stalin had the advantage of being on home ground. He disarmingly made crucial concessions especially over Poland, whose bona fides it was politically impossible to question at the time. The Yalta Declaration on Liberated Europe was to prove worthless. Churchill buoyed himself, as ever, with quantities of champagne which, as one observer remarked, would have ruined the constitution of a lesser man. Back home he tried to put a brave face on the outcome of the Yalta talks, but

With Roosevelt and Stalin, Yalta, February 1945

privately he dreaded what the future might bring for Eastern Europe, and possibly for Europe as a whole.

By the end of April both Hitler and Mussolini were dead. However, Soviet duplicity had already made itself apparent, and Roosevelt too was dead. Churchill urged President Truman to order American forces advancing eastwards on Berlin to make all speed to cover as much territory as possible, and thus keep it from Stalin's Red Army, which had already overrun Eastern Europe, and was poised to capture Berlin. Finally, on 8 May 1945, the fighting in Europe ceased. VE-Day had come at last. In London crowds thronged the streets, hailing Churchill as their saviour. For his part, Churchill was keenly aware that there remained many dangers. Japan fought on in the Far East. The USA would naturally be tempted to withdraw forces from Europe for the Pacific theatre, and this might leave all Europe at Stalin's mercy.

However, the mood in Britain was one of elation. A definite phase of the country's history seemed to have been concluded. Churchill hoped that the Grand Coalition he led might continue in government until the fall of Japan. The Labour leadership agreed, but at the Labour Party Conference the membership insisted on a return to party politics. A General Election was scheduled for 5 July. The result would be delayed for three weeks while the votes of servicemen and women were counted.

Churchill made an ill-judged speech during the campaign in which he warned that a Labour government would not be able to brook democratic opposition, and would eventually resort to 'some form of Gestapo'. This was a terrible thing to say of men who had been his colleagues in the war against Hitler. He remained popular, but such rhetoric inspired little confidence. The result was a landslide for Labour. His wife Clementine, glad that he would now have the chance for some urgently needed rest, observed that it might prove to be a blessing in disguise. He retorted, 'At the moment it seems quite effectively disguised.'

THE ELDER STATESMAN

By common consent Churchill was not an effective Leader of the Opposition. He lacked the patience to wait for his chance to discomfit the government in the Commons. However, he continued to fight for causes he cherished in the international arena, where, even out of office, he commanded more authority than some Prime Ministers have ever done when in it.

February 1946 found him in the USA at President Truman's invitation, to give a lecture in the President's home state of Missouri. In that speech, given at Fulton on 5 March, he warned of the power and the threat of Stalin's USSR.

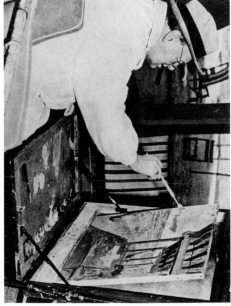

Painting while in the USA, 1946

Already many of the states for whose freedom the Allies had fought were trapped behind an 'iron curtain' (it is some measure of the long-term influence of his analysis that his use of the phrase came to be universally adopted). The only way to friendly settlement was through strength, an effective and powerful United Nations, and a spirit of co-operation between Britain and the USA.

His other great theme in these years was the union of non-communist Europe. His vision was ultimately of a United States of Europe, but he saw clearly that this would have to rest upon the foundation of Franco-German friendship. This entailed putting aside all rancour, and promoting a new Germany, spiritually rejuvenated and with its economy and armed forces rebuilt. At the inaugural meeting of the Council of Europe in 1949 he made the point forcibly by looking about him, as though in surprise, and asking, 'Where are the Germans?'

As a statesman he looked to the future; as an author he dwelt upon the past. As ever he managed to write – in such hours as he snatched from other tasks – more than many a full-time author. He embarked upon his war memoirs, with the additional incentive that the royalties would provide for the comfort of his family. The family was augmented early in 1947 by his daughter, Mary's, marriage to Christopher Soames, then a Guards officer and later an MP, later still a Minister and diplomat. Less than a fortnight later, though, Churchill was cast down by the death of his brother, Jack.

His own health was uncertain. However, when the labour leader, Clement Attlee, called an election for February 1950 he returned to the helm of the Conservative Party. Labour were elected by the narrowest of margins, and formed a minority government. Senior figures in his own party felt that Churchill ought to step aside for a younger man, so that the need to prove himself was added to his burdens. In June 1951

Prime Minister again

he sustained the Opposition during a marathon parliamentary debate of twenty-one hours. The doubting Thomases were wrong-footed. He had the chance to prove himself to the country in the election of October 1951, in which the Conservatives secured a majority of twenty-six.

Almost from the first the possibility of his retirement was being mooted by the Tory élite. Manifestly, Churchill would not lead them into the next election, and it was necessary to establish the new leader as Prime Minister well in advance. Churchill himself indicated that he might only serve for a year, but was determined to re-establish a special relationship with the USA, and to bring the leaders of the USA and the USSR together for a summit meeting (another Churchillian usage that has taken root), to try to bridge the gulf that had opened between East and West. To this end he resumed a life of international diplomacy. These were worthy aims, but made life frustrating for the Prime Minister-elect, Anthony Eden, who was not only Foreign Secretary for the third time in his career, but also had to play second fiddle to a chief who was set upon doing much of the job for him.

For Churchill, it became a race against time to secure this last ambition before his powers faded too greatly. The election of General Eisenhower as President of the USA in November 1952, obliged him to build up a working relationship with a new man; the death of Stalin the following March, however, raised hopes that a new Soviet leader might prove more tractable. Churchill (or rather, Sir Winston, as he became at the insistence of the Queen just before her Coronation), suffered a serious stroke in June 1953. The news of this was not made public, and, determined to bring about the summit conference, he recovered, largely by force of will. In vain. He pursued every chance to promote Soviet-American understanding, but the circumstances of the growing Cold War plucked success from him. On 5 April 1955 he

Sir Winston and Lady Churchill, 1961

resigned as Prime Minister, and was succeeded by Eden.

High office had become necessary to his constitution, and without its stimulus he felt himself ageing more rapidly. He had long been prone to fits of black depression, to which the determination with which he sought excitement, danger and unremitting toil was the counterpart. Now this mighty system, potently compounded of strength of mind and strength of feeling, began to slow. Even so, his retirement was strenuous by ordinary standards. He had won the Nobel Prize for Literature in 1953, and he continued to write, having returned to a project he had begun before the war, *A History of the English-Speaking Peoples*. He spent much of his time in the south of France. He also made the acquaintance of Aristotle Onassis, on whose yacht he was occasionally a guest. He kept on the move, perhaps to push to the back of his mind the feeling that, as he confided to his daughter, Diana, 'My life is over, but it is not yet ended.'

He remained a Member of Parliament, and made his final appearance in the Commons in July 1964 at the age of eighty-nine. His great spirit was freed from its failing body in January 1965 after a terrible stroke. His body lay in state in Westminster Hall, and was accorded a state funeral in St Paul's Cathedral. Churchill's final journey took him by barge to Waterloo, and thence by special train to Bladon in Oxfordshire, where he was buried next to his brother and their parents, barely a mile from Blenheim Palace, where he had been born.

In the preparation of this short life of Churchill I have been particularly indebted to Martin Gilbert's *Churchill: A Life*, and warmly recommend it to anyone wishing to learn more about Churchill.